Essential Guide to Writing

Writing Avenue

Rachel Somer

Paragraph Writing

4

DARAKWON

About the Author

Rachel Somer

BA in English Literature, York University, Toronto, Canada

Award-winning essayist, TOEIC developer, and author of educational books

Over ten years of experience as an English as a Second Language instructor

The author of *Fundamental Reading* Basic 1 and 2

Essential Guide to Writing
Writing Avenue 4
Paragraph Writing

Publisher Chung Kyudo
Author Rachel Somer
Editors Jeong Yeonsoon, Kim Mina, Seo Jeong-ah, Kim Mikyeong
Designers Park Narae, Forest

First published in February 2021
By Darakwon, Inc.
Darakwon Bldg., 211, Munbal-ro, Paju-si, Gyeonggi-do 10881
Republic of Korea
Tel: 82-2-736-2031 (Ext. 250)
Fax: 82-2-732-2037

ISBN 978-89-277-0450-8 54740
978-89-277-0446-1 54740 (set)

www.darakwon.co.kr

Photo Credits
DPeterson (p. 34), Mister_Knight (p. 54), Sean Donohue Photo (p. 54), fritschk (p. 54), Iembi (p. 54), Sean Donohue Photo (p. 56), Takashi Images (p. 56), Anton_Ivanov (p. 57), Proshkin Aleksandr (p. 74), Nussar (p. 74) / www.shutterstock.com
Van_Gogh_-_Starry_Night_-_Google_Art_Project.jpg (p. 84), Mona_Lisa,_by_Leonardo_da_Vinci,_from_C2RMF_retouched.jpg (p. 84), Monet-Mer_agitée_à_Etretat-MBA-Lyon.jpg (p. 84), Edvard-Munch-The-Scream.jpg(p. 84), Sofonisba_Anguissola_001.jpg (p. 84) / https://commons.wikimedia.org

Components Main Book / Workbook
10 9 8 7 6 5 4   24 25 26 27 28

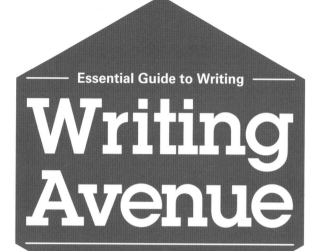

Essential Guide to Writing

Writing Avenue

Paragraph Writing

4

Table of Contents

How to Use This Book

• Student Book

1. Before You Write

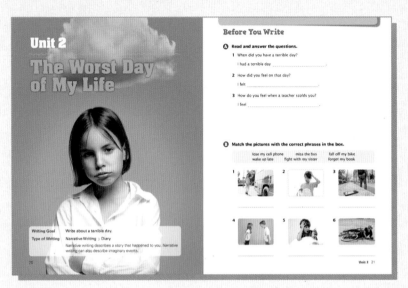

Thinking about the Topic

Three warm-up questions help students think about the writing topic.

Previewing the Key Vocabulary

Students can learn the key vocabulary by matching the words with the pictures or filling in the table.

2. Understanding the Model Text

QR code for listening to the model text

Reading the Model Text

Students can read an example of the writing topic and use it as a template when they write their passage.

Completing the Graphic Organizer

By completing the graphic organizer, students can learn the structure of the model text. This also helps them organize their writing.

A question about the model text is provided.

Completing the Paragraph

By completing the paragraph, students can review the model text and learn what the passage consists of.

3. Collecting Ideas

Getting Ideas from Collecting Ideas

Ideas related to the writing topic are provided. Students can brainstorm and learn new ideas before writing their draft.

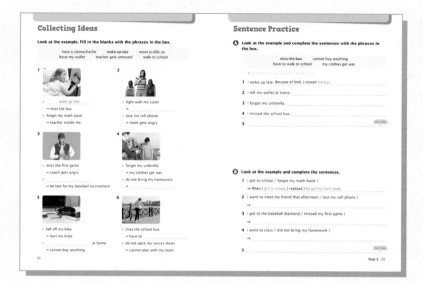

4. Sentence Practice

Practicing Sentences with Key Structures

Various types of questions allow students to practice the key structures of the model text. They also help students gather ideas before writing.

5. Sentence Practice Plus

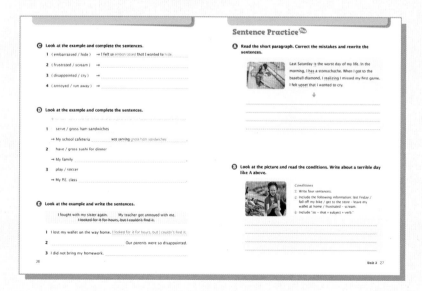

Correcting a Short Paragraph

Students can check if they understand the key structures they learned by correcting the mistakes in the short paragraph.

Writing a Short Paragraph

Students should write a short paragraph by using the given picture and the conditions. This helps students practice the key structures.

6. Brainstorming & First Draft

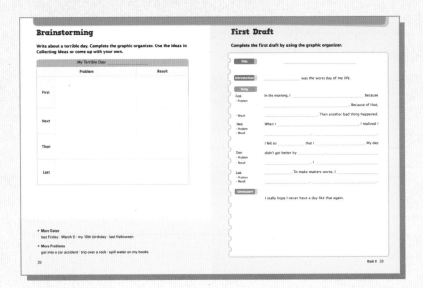

Brainstorming

By completing the graphic organizer, students can organize their ideas prior to writing the first draft.

First Draft

Students should complete the first draft by using the graphic organizer. They can revise, edit the first draft, and write the final draft in the workbook.

Vocabulary and Structure Review

Students can review the key vocabulary they learned in each unit by writing the meaning of each word and phrase. They can also review the key structures in the unit.

• Workbook

7. More Questions

Students can practice and review the key structures. They can also complete the model text by matching the phrases.

8. Revise & Edit ➜ Final Draft

After writing the first draft, students can revise and edit the draft, and then write the final draft.

About Paragraph Writing

1. What Is a Paragraph?

A paragraph is a short piece of writing that handles a single idea or concept. All the sentences in a given paragraph should be related to a single topic. Paragraphs can stand alone, or they can be added to longer pieces of writing such as essays, stories, articles, and many more.

2. What Does a Paragraph Consist of?

A paragraph consists of a topic sentence, supporting details, and a concluding sentence.

– The topic sentence is the main idea of the passage.

– Supporting details are information and examples that explain the topic.

– The concluding sentence is the final thought of the passage.

Topic sentence   **Supporting details**

My Terrible Day

Yesterday was the worst day of my life. In the morning, I woke up late because I forgot to set my alarm. Because of that, I missed the bus. Then another bad thing happened. When I got to school, I realized I forgot my math book. My teacher scolded me in front of the class. I felt so embarrassed that I wanted to hide. My day didn't get better by lunchtime. My school cafeteria was serving gross ham sandwiches. I couldn't eat a bite, so I was hungry all afternoon. To make matters worse, I lost my favorite wallet on the way home. I looked for it for hours, but I couldn't find it. I really hope I never have a day like that again.

Concluding sentence

3. What Are the Types of Paragraph Writing?

1) Expository Writing

It gives information about a topic or tells you how to do something.

2) Narrative Writing

It describes a story that happened to you. It can also describe imaginary events.

3) Persuasive Writing

It encourages a reader to make a choice by providing evidence and examples.

4) Descriptive Writing

It describes a person, place, or thing. It shows what the person, location, or object is like.

Unit 1

My Favorite Time of Day

Writing Goal	Write about your favorite time of day.
Type of Writing	Descriptive Writing 〉 Journal

Descriptive writing describes a person, place, or thing. It shows what the person, location, or object is like.

Before You Write

A **Read and answer the questions.**

1 Do you prefer morning, afternoon, evening, or nighttime?

I prefer _____ .

2 What is your favorite time of day?

My favorite time of day is between _____ and _____ .

3 What do you like to do in your free time?

I like to _____ .

B **Match the pictures with the correct phrases in the box.**

| my favorite club | go jogging | cook dinner |
| at the sky | the school cafeteria | take a walk |

1

7:00 A.M.

_____

2

12:00 P.M

go to _____

3

Between 3:00 and 5:00 P.M.

go to _____

4

Around 6:00 P.M.

_____

5
Around 7:00 P.M.

_____

6

Between 9:00 and 10:00 P.M.

look up _____

Understanding the Model Text

A Read the model text and answer the question.

My Favorite Time: 3:00 to 5:00 P.M.

My favorite time of day is between 3:00 and 5:00 P.M. I finish class around 3:00 P.M. I have some free time before I have to go home and do my homework. Usually, I go to my filmmaking club. I learn how to shoot and edit short films there. Sometimes, when the weather is nice, our film teacher, Mr. Sparks, takes us outside. There is a huge park with many trees, gardens, and fountains near my school. I watch the squirrels chase one another and then film them. I really enjoy being outdoors. After that, I go home and edit my videos while I wait for dinner. I'm glad to have such a relaxing afternoon. It makes me happy and calm.

Q The topic sentence is the main idea of the passage.
Underline the topic sentence.

B Read the model text again and complete the graphic organizer.

Between 3:00 and 5:00 P.M.	
What I Usually Do	• go to my _____ club • learn how to _____ and _____ short films
What I Sometimes Do	• _____ is nice → Mr. Sparks takes us outside • _____ the _____ chase one another and then _____ them
What I Do After That	go home and edit my _____
What I Feel	_____ to have such a _____

C Complete the paragraph by using the model text.

| Title | My Favorite Time: 3:00 to 5:00 P.M. |

Introduction

My favorite time of day is between _____.

I _____. I have some free time before

I _____.

Body

What I Usually Do

Usually, I _____. I _____

What I Sometimes Do

_____. Sometimes,

when _____.

There _____.

I watch _____.

What I Do After That

I really enjoy _____. After that, I _____

_____ while _____.

Conclusion

What I Feel

I'm _____ to have such _____.

It makes me _____.

Collecting Ideas

Look at the example. Fill in the blanks with the phrases in the box.

> go to the school cafeteria   ~~film the squirrels in the park~~   go to the gym
> watch meteors fly   watch cooking videos   have our soccer match

1

- Between 3:00 and 5:00 P.M.
- go to my filmmaking club
- film the squirrels in the park

2

- Between 7:00 and 8:00 A.M.
- _____
- go jogging in the park

3

- Between 12:00 and 1:00 P.M.
- _____
- take a walk in the school garden

4

- Between 4:00 and 5:00 P.M.
- go to the soccer field
- _____

  in the school gym

5

- Between 6:00 and 8:00 P.M.
- stay in my room and

  _____
- cook dinner for my family

6

- Between 8:00 and 10:00 P.M.
- go to the balcony in my house
- _____

  across the sky

Sentence Practice

A **Look at the pictures and write the sentences.**

I stay in my room   ~~I go to my filmmaking club~~
I go to the balcony in my house   I go to the school cafeteria

1   I go to my filmmaking club.

I learn how to shoot and edit short films.

2   _____

I watch cooking videos on YouTube.

3   _____

I look up at the beautiful night sky.

4   _____

I have lunch and chat with my friends.

5   Your Idea   _____

B **Look at the example and complete the sentences.**

1 (weather / nice)

→   **When the** weather **is** nice,   our film teacher takes us outside.

2 (sky / clear)

→   _____   I look through my telescope.

3 (weather / nice)

→   _____   we go outside after lunch.

4 (my parents / tired)

→   _____   I cook dinner for my family.

Your Idea

5 _____

C Look at the example and complete the sentences.

Use "is" for one noun, and use "are" for a group of nouns.

1 (a huge park / near my school)

→ **There is** a huge park near my school.

2 (a small garden / in the school)

→ _____

3 (many planets, moons, and beautiful stars / in space)

→ _____

D Look at the example and rewrite the sentences.

1 I watch the squirrels. They chase one another.

→ I **watch** the squirrels **chase** one another.

2 I watch small meteors. They fly across the sky.

→ _____

3 I hear my friends. They cheer for me.

→ _____

E Look at the example and complete the sentences.

1 I / edit my videos / wait for dinner

→ I edit my videos **while I** wait for dinner.

2 I / think about the stars / get ready for bed

→ _____

3 I / think about the game / my mom / prepare dinner

→ _____

Sentence Practice ^{Plus}

A Read the short paragraph. Correct the mistakes and rewrite the sentences.

My favorite time of day is <u>in</u> 7:00 and 8:00 A.M. When the weather is nice, I <u>went</u> jogging in the park. I hear the birds <u>to sing</u> in the trees. After that, I take a shower while my dad <u>made</u> breakfast.

_____

_____

_____

_____

B Look at the picture and read the conditions. Write about your favorite time of day like A above.

Conditions

① Write four sentences.

② Include the following information: 12:00 and 1:00 P.M. / take a walk – school garden / watch the butterflies / fly in the garden / listen to music / wait for my next class.

③ Include "watch + object + verb" and "while."

_____

_____

_____

_____

Brainstorming

Write about your favorite time of day. Complete the graphic organizer. Use the ideas in Collecting Ideas or come up with your own.

My Favorite Time: _____	
What I Usually Do	• •
What I Sometimes Do	• •
What I Do After That	
What I Feel	

◆ **More Places to Go**

book club / library / basketball court / dance class / swimming pool

◆ **More Things to Do**

discuss the story / borrow some books / watch the game / practice a new dance / practice diving

First Draft

Complete the first draft by using the graphic organizer.

Title _____

Introduction

My favorite time of day is between _____.

I _____. I have some free time

before I _____.

Body

What I Usually Do

Usually, I _____. I _____

What I Sometimes Do

_____. Sometimes,

when _____.

There _____.

I _____. I really

What I Do After That

enjoy _____. After that, I _____

_____ while _____

_____.

Conclusion

What I Feel

I'm _____ to have such _____.

It makes me _____.

Unit 2
The Worst Day of My Life

Writing Goal	Write about a terrible day.
Type of Writing	Narrative Writing » Diary
	Narrative writing describes a story that happened to you. Narrative writing can also describe imaginary events.

Before You Write

A **Read and answer the questions.**

1 When did you have a terrible day?

I had a terrible day _____.

2 How did you feel on that day?

I felt _____.

3 How do you feel when a teacher scolds you?

I feel _____.

B **Match the pictures with the correct phrases in the box.**

lose my cell phone	miss the bus	fall off my bike
wake up late	fight with my sister	forget my book

1

_____

2

_____

3

_____

4

_____

5

_____

6

_____

Understanding the Model Text

A **Read the model text and answer the question.**

My Terrible Day

Yesterday was the worst day of my life. In the morning, I woke up late because I forgot to set my alarm. Because of that, I missed the bus. Then another bad thing happened. When I got to school, I realized I forgot my math book. My teacher scolded me in front of the class. I felt so embarrassed that I wanted to hide. My day didn't get better by lunchtime. My school cafeteria was serving gross ham sandwiches. I couldn't eat a bite, so I was hungry all afternoon. To make matters worse, I lost my favorite wallet on the way home. I looked for it for hours, but I couldn't find it. I really hope I never have a day like that again.

Q The concluding sentence is the final thought of the passage. Underline the concluding sentence.

B **Read the model text again and complete the graphic organizer.**

My Terrible Day		
	Problem	**Result**
First	_____ late because I forgot to set my alarm	missed the _____
Next	realized I forgot my _____	teacher _____ me
Then	school cafeteria was serving gross _____	_____ a bite
Last	lost my favorite _____	couldn't _____ it

C **Complete the paragraph by using the model text.**

My Terrible Day

Introduction

_____ was the worst day of my life.

Body

First
- Problem

In the _____, I _____ because _____

- Result

_____. Because of that, I _____.

Next

Then _____ bad thing happened. When I _____

- Problem

_____, I realized I _____.

- Result

_____.

I felt so _____ that I _____.

Then
- Problem
- Result

My day didn't get better by _____. _____

_____. I _____,

so I _____. To make matters worse,

Last
- Problem
- Result

I _____.

_____.

Conclusion

I really hope I never have a day like that again.

Collecting Ideas

Look at the example. Fill in the blanks with the phrases in the box.

have a stomachache	~~wake up late~~	mom scolds us
leave my wallet	teacher gets annoyed	walk to school

1

- _____wake up late_____
  → miss the bus
- forget my math book
  → teacher scolds me

2

- fight with my sister
  → _____
- lose my cell phone
  → mom gets angry

3

- miss the first game
  → coach gets angry
- _____
  → be late for my baseball tournament

4

- forget my umbrella
  → my clothes get wet
- do not bring my homework
  → _____

5

- fall off my bike
  → hurt my knee
- _____ at home
  → cannot buy anything

6

- miss the school bus
  → have to _____
- do not pack my soccer shoes
  → cannot play with my team

Sentence Practice

A **Look at the example and complete the sentences with the phrases in the box.**

> ~~miss the bus~~   cannot buy anything
> have to walk to school   my clothes get wet

Remember to change the verbs to the past tense.

1 I woke up late. **Because of that, I missed** the bus. _____

2 I left my wallet at home. _____

3 I forgot my umbrella. _____

4 I missed the school bus. _____

5 _____ `Your Idea`

B **Look at the example and complete the sentences.**

1 (got to school / forgot my math book)

→ **When I** got to school, **I realized I** forgot my math book. _____

2 (went to meet my friend that afternoon / lost my cell phone)

→ _____

3 (got to the baseball diamond / missed my first game)

→ _____

4 (went to class / did not bring my homework)

→ _____

5 _____ `Your Idea`

C Look at the example and complete the sentences.

1 (embarrassed / hide) → I felt so embarrassed **that I wanted to** hide.

2 (frustrated / scream) → _____

3 (disappointed / cry) → _____

4 (annoyed / run away) → _____

D Look at the example and complete the sentences.

💡 Use "was / were + verb-ing" to talk about an ongoing action that happened at some point in the past.

1 serve / gross ham sandwiches

→ My school cafeteria _____ **was serving** gross ham sandwiches _____ .

2 have / gross sushi for dinner

→ My family _____ .

3 play / soccer

→ My P.E. class _____ .

E Look at the example and write the sentences.

I fought with my sister again.   My teacher got annoyed with me.
~~I looked for it for hours, but I couldn't find it.~~

1 I lost my wallet on the way home. I looked for it for hours, but I couldn't find it.

2 _____ Our parents were so disappointed.

3 I did not bring my homework. _____

Sentence Practice ^{Plus}

Ⓐ **Read the short paragraph. Correct the mistakes and rewrite the sentences.**

Last Saturday <u>is</u> the worst day of my life. In the morning, I <u>has</u> a stomachache. When I got to the baseball diamond, I <u>realizing</u> I missed my first game. I felt <u>upset</u> that I wanted to cry.

_____

_____

_____

_____

Ⓑ **Look at the picture and read the conditions. Write about a terrible day like A above.**

Conditions

① Write four sentences.

② Include the following information: last Friday / fall off my bike / get to the store – leave my wallet at home / frustrated – scream.

③ Include "so ~ that + subject + verb."

_____

_____

_____

_____

Brainstorming

Write about a terrible day. Complete the graphic organizer. Use the ideas in Collecting Ideas or come up with your own.

My Terrible Day: _____		
	Problem	**Result**
First		
Next		
Then		
Last		

- **More Dates**

  last Friday / March 5 / my 10th birthday / last Halloween

- **More Problems**

  get into a car accident / trip over a rock / spill water on my books

First Draft

Complete the first draft by using the graphic organizer.

Title

_____

Introduction

_____ was the worst day of my life.

Body

First
- Problem

In the morning, I _____ because

_____. Because of that,

- Result

_____. Then another bad thing happened.

Next
- Problem
- Result

When I _____, I realized I

_____. _____.

I felt so _____ that I _____. My day

Then
- Problem

didn't get better by _____. _____

- Result

_____. I _____

Last
- Problem

_____. To make matters worse, I _____

- Result

_____. _____.

Conclusion

I really hope I never have a day like that again.

Unit 3

School Lunches Around the World

Writing Goal	Write about school lunch in another country.
Type of Writing	Expository Writing » Report
	Expository writing gives information about a topic or tells you how to do something.

Before You Write

A **Read and answer the questions.**

1 Do you like your school's cafeteria food?

☐ Yes, I do.   ☐ No, I don't.

2 Where do you eat lunch at school?

I eat lunch _____ .

3 What do you like to eat for lunch?

I like to eat _____ for lunch.

B **Match the pictures with the correct words and phrases in the box.**

dessert	meat and vegetables	baked goods
sandwich	healthy salad	rice and soup

1

_____

2

_____

3

_____

4

_____

5

_____

6

_____

Understanding the Model Text

A **Read the model text and answer the question.**

School Lunch in France

What do you normally eat for lunch at school? In France, students eat nutritious foods to stay healthy. French students usually have salad, meat, vegetables, and some dessert. They have lunch in the school cafeteria. The food is served on a tray. First, students eat a healthy salad. The salad is made with cucumbers, cabbage, and tomatoes. Then, students eat meat and vegetables. For example, they might have fish, sausages, or beef that is covered in sauce. Lastly, the students get dessert. Sometimes they have fruit, such as apples or peaches. Other times they eat something sweet, like ice cream, cake, or apple pie. The students love these tasty desserts. After lunch, they feel full, and they are ready to study again!

Q What is the passage mainly about?
 a. lunch foods in French schools
 b. where French students eat lunch

B **Read the model text again and complete the graphic organizer.**

School Lunch in France	
Place	in the _____
First	• eat a healthy _____ - made with _____, cabbage, and _____
Then	• eat _____ and vegetables - fish, sausages, or _____ that _____ in sauce
Last	• get _____ - fruit: apples or peaches - something sweet: ice cream, cake, or _____

C Complete the paragraph by using the model text.

Title	School Lunch in France

Introduction

What do you normally eat for lunch at school? In _____,

students eat _____ foods _____ stay _____.

Body

_____ students usually have _____

Place   _____. They have lunch _____.

First   The food is served _____. First, students eat _____

- Ingredients   _____. _____ made with _____

Then   _____. Then, students eat _____

_____. For example, they might have _____

Last   _____ that _____. Lastly, the students get

_____. Sometimes they have _____, such as

_____. Other times they _____

_____. The students love _____

_____.

Conclusion

After lunch, they feel _____, and they are ready to study

again!

Collecting Ideas

Look at the example. Fill in the blanks with the phrases in the box.

rice and soup   cutlets and potatoes   a sandwich
~~beef and vegetables~~   fried corn cakes   grilled fish or tofu

1

France

- a healthy salad
- fish, sausages, or
  <u>beef and vegetables</u>
- fruit, ice cream, cake, or apple pie

2

The U.S.

- _____
- vegetables
- chocolate milk, ice cream, or baked goods

3

South Korea

- _____
- fish, fried chicken, or pork and side dishes
- fruit, cookies, or yogurt

4

Colombia

- rice and beans
- meatballs or chicken, vegetables, and plantains
- fresh juice or _____

5

Japan

- rice and soup
- _____ and vegetables
- fruit or milk

6

Ukraine

- soup called borscht
- sausages or _____
- biscuits, pancakes, or cream cheese

Sentence Practice

A **Look at the example and complete the sentences.**

1 (France / nutritious / healthy)

→ In France, **students eat** nutritious **foods to stay** healthy.

2 (South Korea / healthy / strong)

→ _____

3 (the U.S. / delicious / full all afternoon)

→ _____

4 (Colombia / nutritious / healthy)

→ _____

Your Idea

5 _____

B **Look at the example and complete the sentences.**

The U.S. → American | Korea → Korean | Ukraine → Ukrainian

1 France – salad, meat, vegetables, some dessert

→ **French students usually have** salad, meat, vegetables, **and** some dessert.

2 The U.S. – sandwiches, vegetables, some dessert

→ _____

3 South Korea – rice, soup, meat, side dishes, some dessert

→ _____

4 Ukraine – borscht, sausages, some dessert

→ _____

Your Idea

5 _____

C Look at the pictures. Complete the sentences with the phrases in the box.

red beets, meat, corn, and potatoes	~~cucumbers, cabbage, and tomatoes~~
bread, cheese, lettuce, and avocados	soy sauce, tofu, and some vegetables

1 The salad **is made with** cucumbers, cabbage, and tomatoes   .

2 The sandwich   .

3 The soup   .

4 The soup   .

D Look at the example and complete the sentences.

(fish, sausages) (beef covered in sauce)

→ **They might have** fish, sausages, **or** beef **that is** covered in sauce.

💡 Use "is" for singular or uncountable nouns. Use "are" for plural nouns.

1 (carrots, peas, broccoli) (beans cooked in sauce)

→ _____

2 (fish, fried chicken) (pork covered in sauce)

→ _____

3 (soup, stew) (curry served on rice)

→ _____

4 (meatballs, chicken) (plantains fried in oil)

→ _____

Sentence Practice Plus

A **Read the short paragraph. Correct the mistakes and rewrite the sentences.**

In Colombia, students eat nutritious foods to <u>staying</u> healthy. First, they eat rice and beans. Then, students <u>eats</u> meat and vegetables. For example, they might have meatballs, chicken, or plantains that <u>is</u> fried in oil.

_____

_____

_____

_____

B **Look at the picture and read the conditions. Write about school lunch in South Korea like A above.**

Conditions

① Write four sentences.

② Include the following information: healthy / strong / rice and soup / meat, side dishes / fish, fried chicken, or pork – covered in sauce.

③ Include a to-infinitive of purpose and the relative pronoun "that."

_____

_____

_____

_____

Brainstorming

Write about school lunch in another country. Complete the graphic organizer. Use the ideas in Collecting Ideas or come up with your own.

School Lunch _____	
Place	
First	• ___
Then	• ___
Last	• ___ ___

• **More Places to Eat**

in the classroom / in the schoolyard

• **More Countries and Foods**

India (curried lentils, vegetables, and roti) / Italy (salad, meat, and pasta or risotto) / Norway (sandwiches, yogurt, and fruit)

First Draft

Complete the first draft by using the graphic organizer.

Title

_____

Introduction

What do you normally eat for lunch at school? In _____, students eat _____ foods _____ stay _____ _____.

Body

_____ students usually have _____

Place   _____. They have lunch _____.

First   The food is served _____. First, students eat

- Ingredients   _____. _____ made with

Then   _____. Then, students eat _____. For example, they might have _____ _____ that _____.

Last   Lastly, the students get _____. Sometimes they have _____, such as _____.

Other times they _____.

The students love _____.

Conclusion

After lunch, they feel _____, and they are ready to study again!

Unit 4
The Most Popular Pets

Writing Goal	Write about your classmates' favorite pets.
Type of Writing	Expository Writing » Survey
	Expository writing gives information about a topic or tells you how to do something.

Before You Write

A **Read and answer the questions.**

1 Do you have a pet?

☐ Yes, I do.   ☐ No, I don't.

2 If you could have a pet, what would you choose?

I would get a(n) _____ .

3 In your opinion, what pets are easy to take care of?

I think _____ are easy to take care of.

B **Fill in the chart with the words and phrases in the box.**

| interesting | noisy at night | difficult to feed |
| scary | friendly and playful | quiet and beautiful |

I like them because they are ...	I don't like them because they are ...
• _____	• _____
• _____	• _____
• _____	• _____

Understanding the Model Text

A Read the model text and answer the question.

My Classmates' Favorite Pets

Everyone in my class wants a pet. I asked my classmates which pets they like the most. Here are the results of the survey. This chart shows that fifteen students voted for dogs. They said dogs are the friendliest and most playful pets. This makes dogs the most popular. Cats are the second most popular pets. Nine students like cats the best because they are easy to take care of. You don't need to walk a cat or play with it a lot. Next, five students voted for hamsters. However, most students don't like hamsters because they are noisy at night. What is the least popular pet? Snakes! Only two students voted for snakes. The rest of the class said snakes are scary and difficult to feed.

Q What is the passage mainly about?
   a. the worst pets to own
   b. opinions about pets

B Read the model text again and complete the graphic organizer.

Favorite Pets			
Pets	Popularity	Votes	Reason
Dogs	most popular	15	the _____ and most playful
Cats	_____ most popular	9	• easy to _____ • don't need to _____ or play with it a lot
Hamsters	third most popular	_____	_____ at night
Snakes	_____ popular	2	scary and difficult _____

C **Complete the paragraph by using the model text.**

Title	My Classmates' Favorite Pets

Introduction

Everyone in my class _____ a pet. I asked my classmates _____ pets they like _____. Here are the _____ of the survey.

Body

Most Popular

This chart shows that _____ students voted for _____.

- Reason

They said _____.

Second Most Popular

This makes _____ the most popular. _____ are the _____ most popular pets. _____ like _____ the best because _____.

- Reason

_____.

Third Most Popular

Next, _____ voted for _____. However,

- Reason

most students don't _____ because _____ _____.

Conclusion

Least Popular

What is the least popular pet? _____! Only _____

- Reason

_____ voted for _____. The rest of the class said _____.

Collecting Ideas

Look at the example. Fill in the blanks with the phrases in the box.

noisy at night	easy to feed	slimy and boring
hard to play with	fun to watch	~~friendly and playful~~

Good Points

Bad Points

1

- Dogs: ___friendly and playful___
- Cats: easy to take care of

4

- Snakes: scary and difficult to feed
- Spiders: scary and

_____

2

- Fish: quiet and beautiful
- Rabbits: small and

_____

5

- Hamsters: _____
- Turtles: smell bad

3

- Birds: _____
- Iguanas: quiet and interesting

6

- Scorpions: scary and dangerous
- Snails: _____

Sentence Practice

A Look at the example and complete the sentences.

1 (fifteen / dogs)

→ **This chart shows that** fifteen **students voted for** dogs.

2 (seventeen / fish)

→ _____

3 (eleven / iguanas)

→ _____

4 (twenty / rabbits)

→ _____

Your Idea

5 _____

B Look at the example and rewrite the sentences.

They said dogs are friendly and playful pets.
→ They said dogs are **the friendliest** and **most** playful pets.

💡 Change the adjectives to the superlative form by adding -est or most.

1 They said fish are quiet and beautiful pets.

→ They said fish are _____ .

2 They said cats are cute and smart pets.

→ They said cats are _____ .

3 They said rabbits are soft and furry pets.

→ They said rabbits are _____ .

Your Idea

4 _____

C Look at the example and complete the sentences.

1 (cat / second most) → **Cats are the** second most **popular pets**. _____

2 (snake / least) → _____

3 (fish / most) → _____

4 (rabbit / second most) → _____

D Look at the example and complete the sentences.

💡 To-infinitives can act as adverbs and modify adjectives.

1 | they / easy / take care of |

→ Nine students like cats the best ____ **because** they **are** easy **to** take care of ____ .

2 | they / easy / feed |

→ Ten students like rabbits the best _____ .

3 | their cages / easy / clean |

→ Twelve students like iguanas the best _____ .

E Look at the pictures and complete the sentences.

💡 Use a plural noun when referring to a group of animals.

1 (are noisy at night)

→ **Most students don't like** hamsters **because they** are noisy at night. ____

2 (smell bad)

→ _____

3 (are hard to play with)

→ _____

46

Sentence Practice Plus

A **Read the short paragraph. Correct the mistakes and rewrite the sentences.**

This chart shows that eighteen students <u>vote</u> for cats. They said cats are the <u>cute</u> and <u>most smart</u> pets. Twelve students like iguanas the best because their cages are easy <u>for</u> clean.

_____

_____

_____

B **Look at the picture and read the conditions. Write about the most popular pets like A above.**

Conditions

① Write three sentences.

② Include the following information: twenty students / rabbits – soft and furry / eight students / dogs – easy, play with.

③ Include two superlative adjectives and "adjective + to-infinitive."

_____

_____

_____

Brainstorming

Write about your classmates' favorite pets. Complete the graphic organizer. Use the ideas in Collecting Ideas or come up with your own.

My Classmates' _____			
Pets	Popularity	Votes	Reason

• **More Pets**

   parrots / snails / guinea pigs / ferrets / hedgehogs

• **More Superlatives**

   smallest / fastest / most dangerous / strangest / prettiest

First Draft

Complete the first draft by using the graphic organizer.

Title

_____

Introduction

Everyone in my class wants _____. I asked my

classmates _____ pets they like _____.

Here are the _____ of the survey.

Body

Most Popular

This chart shows that _____ students voted _____.

- Reason

They said _____.

Second Most
Popular

This makes _____ the most popular. _____ are the

_____ most popular pets. _____ like

- Reason

_____ the best because _____

_____. _____.

Third Most Popular

Next, _____ voted for _____. However, most

- Reason

students _____ because _____

_____.

Conclusion

Least Popular

What is the least popular pet? _____! Only _____

- Reason

_____ voted for _____. The rest of the class said

_____.

Unit 5

The Best Place to Travel

Writing Goal	Recommend a place to go on vacation.
Type of Writing	Persuasive Writing » Letter
	Persuasive writing encourages a reader to make a choice by providing evidence and examples.

Before You Write

A **Read and answer the questions.**

1 Have you ever traveled to another country?

☐ Yes, I have.   ☐ No, I haven't.

2 Where did you go on your last vacation?

I went to _____.

3 Who did you travel with?

I went there with _____.

B **Fill in the chart with the words in the box.**

temple	a tour	a contest	palace
visit	market	museum	photographs

Places to Visit	Things to Do
• _____	• take _____
• _____	• go on _____
• _____	• take part in _____
• _____	• _____ a botanic garden

Understanding the Model Text

A **Read the model text and answer the question.**

You Should Visit Cambodia

Hi, Jessica,

Are you going to take a trip this year? I suggest you visit Cambodia. I have been there once with my parents. It was a wonderful trip. While I was there, I visited Angkor Wat. It is one of the most famous landmarks in Cambodia. We saw a lot of beautiful temples there. It took all day to walk through the park. You should go there at sunrise or sunset. That's the best time to take photographs. Next, we went to the Old Market. It is the most crowded market in Phnom Penh. You can buy vegetables, seafood, clothes, and even motorcycles there. I suggest you try the fish amok. It is a steamed coconut fish. My family loved it, so we ate it every day.

Your friend,

Jerry

Q What is the passage mainly about?
a. reasons to go to Cambodia   b. things to eat in Cambodia

B **Read the model text again and complete the graphic organizer.**

Cambodia	
Place 1: Angkor Wat	**Place 2: The Old Market**
one of the most famous _____	the most _____ market in Phnom Penh
• What We Did - saw a lot of beautiful _____ - took _____ to walk through the park	• What You Can Do - buy vegetables, seafood, clothes, and _____
• Suggestion - go at _____ or _____	• Suggestion - try the fish amok

C Complete the paragraph by using the model text.

Title
You Should Visit Cambodia

Introduction

Hi, _____,

Are you going to take a trip _____? I suggest you visit

Number of times
I have been there
_____. I have _____ with _____.

It was _____ trip.

Body

Place 1
- What We Did
While I was there, I _____. It is _____

_____ in _____. We _____

_____. It took _____ to _____

- Suggestion
_____. You should go there _____

_____. That's the best time to _____.

Place 2
Next, we _____. It is _____

- What You Can Do
in _____. You can _____

- Suggestion
_____ there. I suggest you

_____. _____.

My _____, so _____.

Conclusion

Your friend,

_____

Collecting Ideas

Look at the example. Fill in the blanks with the phrases in the box.

~~see beautiful temples~~	rock formations	try the hot crepes
see kangaroos and koalas	a sand sculpture contest	take a tour

1

 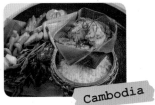

Cambodia

- Angkor Wat
- <u>see beautiful temples</u>

- The Old Market
- try the fish amok

2

France

- The Palace of Versailles
- go on a tour of the palace

- Bastille Market
- _____

3

Egypt

- The Giza Pyramid Complex
- see the pyramids

- White Desert National Park
- photograph the

  _____

4

The U.S.

- Texas SandFest
- take part in

  _____

- The Seafood Market
- try the fresh lobster

5

Italy

- The Colosseum
- _____ of the arena

- The Vatican Museums
- see the Sistine Chapel

6

Australia

- Kangaroo Island
- _____

- Adelaide
- visit the Adelaide Botanic Garden

Sentence Practice

A **Look at the example and complete the sentences.**

be / there once with my parents
→ **I have been** there once with my parents.

💡 Remember to change the verb to the present perfect tense (have p.p.).

1 travel / there twice with my family

→ _____

2 visit / her three times this year

→ _____

3 be / to France a few times

→ _____

Your Idea

4 _____

B **Look at the pictures. Complete the sentences with the phrases in the box.**

~~famous landmark in Cambodia~~   good outdoor market in Paris
famous tourist attraction in Italy   unique place in Australia

1 Angkor Wat

It is one of the most famous **landmarks** in Cambodia.

2 The Colosseum

_____

3 Bastille Market

_____

4 Kangaroo Island

_____

C **Look at the pictures. Complete the sentences with the words in the box.**

~~see~~
go on
see
take part in

~~a lot of beautiful temples~~
the pyramids and the Great Sphinx
the sand sculpture contest
a tour of the palace

💡 Remember to change the verb to the past tense.

1 We _____ **saw** a lot of beautiful temples _____ there.

2 We _____ there.

3 We _____ there.

4 We _____ there.

D **Look at the example and complete the sentences.**

💡 Use "It is a(n) ..." with a singular noun and "They are ..." with plural nouns.

1 (try the fish amok) (a steamed coconut fish)

→ **I suggest you** try the fish amok. **It is** a steamed coconut fish.

2 (try the hot crepes) (thin, sweet pancakes)

→ _____

3 (see the Sistine Chapel) (a beautiful old chapel with many paintings)

→ _____

4 (visit the Adelaide Botanic Garden) (a huge park with many gardens)

→ _____

Sentence Practice Plus

A **Read the short paragraph. Correct the mistakes and rewrite the sentences.**

 I suggest you <u>visiting</u> Egypt. I have <u>be</u> there twice with my family. We <u>go</u> to White Desert National Park. I suggest you <u>photographed</u> the rock formations.

_____

_____

_____

_____

B **Look at the picture and read the conditions. Write about Italy as if you have been there like A above.**

Conditions

① Write four sentences.

② Include the following information: three times – my parents / the Vatican Museums / see the Sistine Chapel.

③ Include the present perfect tense and "I suggest."

_____

_____

_____

_____

Brainstorming

Recommend a place to go on vacation. Complete the graphic organizer. Use the ideas in Collecting Ideas or come up with your own.

You Should Visit _____	
Place 1: _____	Place 2: _____
What We Did	What You Can Do
Suggestion	Suggestion

◆ **More Places to Go**

Germany – the Brandenburg Gate / Canada – Niagara Falls / India – the Taj Mahal / China – the Ice and Snow Festival

First Draft

Complete the first draft by using the graphic organizer.

Title _____

Introduction

Hi, _____,

Are you going to take a trip _____? I suggest

Number of times I have been there

you visit _____. I have _____

_____. It was _____ trip.

Body

Place 1
- What We Did

While I was there, I _____.

It is _____.

We _____. It took _____

- Suggestion

to _____. You should go there

_____. That's the best time to _____

Place 2

_____. Next, we _____.

It is _____.

- What You Can Do

You can _____.

- Suggestion

I suggest you _____. _____

_____. My _____,

so _____.

Conclusion

Your friend,

_____

Unit 6

Save the Environment

Writing Goal	Write about ways to save the environment.
Type of Writing	Expository Writing » Science Poster
	Expository writing gives information about a topic or tells you how to do something.

Before You Write

A **Read and answer the questions.**

1 Do you recycle cans, bottles, and paper?

☐ Yes, I do. ☐ No, I don't.

2 What is one type of pollution?

_____ is a type of pollution.

3 What can you do to save energy?

I can _____ .

B **Match the pictures with the correct phrases in the box.**

save water   reduce food waste   reduce garbage
save paper   save energy   reduce air pollution

1

_____

2

_____

3

_____

4

_____

5

_____

6

_____

Understanding the Model Text

A **Read the model text and answer the question.**

Let's Reduce Pollution

Pollution is a big problem all over the world. Let's help save our Earth. Take a look at my poster. Here are two ways you can save the environment. First, you should reduce the amount of garbage you make. To do that, you should recycle as much as possible. Wash and separate your recycling before you put it outside. In addition, don't buy so much plastic. Why don't you bring your own bags when you shop? Second, you should save energy. When you leave a room, turn off the lights. Remember to turn off computers and televisions if you aren't using them. In winter, lower the heat and put on a sweater. These are just two ways you can help the environment.

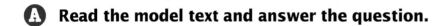

Q What is the passage mainly about?
a. problems with the environment
b. ways to help the environment

B **Read the model text again and complete the graphic organizer.**

Reduce Pollution	
Solution 1	Solution 2
reduce the amount of _____	_____
• _____ as much as possible - wash and separate your recycling • don't buy so much _____ • bring _____ when you shop	• leave a room ➙ turn off the lights • _____ and televisions • lower the heat and _____ in winter

C Complete the paragraph by using the model text.

Title

Let's Reduce Pollution

Introduction

Pollution is a _____ all over the world. Let's help save

our Earth. Take a look _____. Here are two ways

you can _____.

Body

Solution 1

First, you should _____.

- Examples

To do that, you should _____. _____

_____. In addition,

_____. Why don't you _____

Solution 2

_____? Second, you should _____

- Examples

_____. When you _____.

Remember _____

_____. _____

_____.

Conclusion

These are just two _____ you can help the environment.

Collecting Ideas

Look at the example. Fill in the blanks with the phrases in the box.

put food away	turn off the lights	take shorter showers
public transportation	a reusable bottle or cup	~~buy so much plastic~~

1

- Reduce Garbage
- recycle as much as possible
- don't ___buy so much plastic___

2

- Save Energy
- leave a room
  - → _____
- turn off computers and televisions

3

- Reduce Air Pollution
- take _____
- walk to school or ride your bike

4

- Save Water
- wash the dishes
  - → try to use less water
- _____

5

- Reduce Food Waste
- don't buy so much at the grocery store
- _____ properly

6

- Save Paper
- take notes → use recycled paper
- bring _____ to school

64

Sentence Practice

A **Look at the example and rewrite the sentences.**

> You make garbage. You should reduce the amount of garbage.
> → You should reduce the amount of **garbage you make.**

> 🌵 The relative pronoun "that" can be omitted when it acts as an object.

1 You make air pollution. You should reduce the amount of air pollution.

→ _____

2 You waste food. You should reduce the amount of food.

→ _____

3 You make water pollution. You should reduce the amount of water pollution.

→ _____

Your Idea

4 _____

B **Look at the example and rewrite the sentences.**

> 🌵 Use "why don't you + verb ~?" when you make a suggestion.

1 Bring your own bags when you shop.

→ **Why don't you** bring your own bags when you shop**?**

2 Ask your family to take the bus sometimes instead of driving.

→ _____

3 Save the leftovers in the refrigerator after cooking.

→ _____

4 Use cold water instead of hot when you do your laundry.

→ _____

Your Idea

5 _____

C Look at the example and complete the sentences with the phrases in the box.

> buy only
> take a bus or the subway
> ~~wash and separate your recycling~~
>
> instead of a car
> what you need for the week
> ~~before you put it outside~~

1 You should recycle as much as possible.

Wash and separate your recycling before you put it outside.

2 You should take public transportation.

_____

3 You should not buy so much at the grocery store.

_____

D Look at the example and complete the sentences.

> ~~turn off the lights~~   buy recyclable items   try to use less water

1 When you leave a room, _____ turn off the lights _____ .

2 When you wash the dishes, _____ .

3 When you go shopping, _____ .

E Look at the example and rewrite the sentences.

1 Turn off computers and televisions if you aren't using them.

→ **Remember to** turn off computers and televisions if you aren't using them.

2 Take shorter showers, too.

→ _____

3 Use natural shampoos and soaps.

→ _____

Sentence Practice Plus

A **Read the short paragraph. Correct the mistakes and rewrite the sentences.**

Here are two <u>way</u> you can save the environment. First, you should reduce the amount of food you <u>wasting</u>. Second, you should <u>saving</u> paper. Remember <u>bring</u> a reusable bottle or cup to school.

_____

_____

_____

_____

B **Look at the picture and read the conditions. Write about two ways to help save the environment like A above.**

Conditions

① Write four sentences.

② Include the following information: reduce water pollution / use green products / use natural shampoos and soaps.

③ Include a sentence that omits the relative pronoun "that." Include "remember to + verb."

_____

_____

_____

_____

Brainstorming

Write about two ways to save the environment. Complete the graphic organizer. Use the ideas in Collecting Ideas or come up with your own.

Let's _____	
Solution 1	Solution 2
•	•
•	•
•	•

More Ways to Save the Environment

plant trees / turn old items into something new / donate old clothes and toys / buy used electronics / never use paper cups

First Draft

Complete the first draft by using the graphic organizer.

Title _____

Introduction

Pollution is _____ all over the world. Let's help

save our Earth. Take a look _____. Here are two

_____ you can _____.

Body

Solution 1

First, you should _____.

- Examples

To do that, you should _____.

_____. In addition,

_____. Why don't you

_____?

Solution 2

Second, you should _____. When you

- Examples

_____. Remember

_____.

_____.

Conclusion

These are just two ways you can help _____.

Unit 7

Join Us at the Fair

Writing Goal	Write an announcement for a special event.
Type of Writing	Persuasive Writing Announcement
	Persuasive writing encourages a reader to make a choice by providing evidence and examples.

Before You Write

A **Read and answer the questions.**

1 Have you ever been to a festival?

☐ Yes, I have.   ☐ No, I haven't.

2 Where was the festival?

It was _____.

3 What did you do there?

I _____.

B **Fill in the chart with the phrases in the box.**

school fair   ice festival   watch plays   go on rides
see artwork   art exhibition   sports day   meet musicians

Events	Activities
• _____	• _____
• _____	• _____
• _____	• _____
• _____	• _____

Understanding the Model Text

A Read the model text and answer the question.

Announcement: School Fair

Come and join us at the Oak School Fair. ★ There will be fun for the whole family. You can go on rides or play some games. Enjoy delicious snacks, such as cotton candy 🍭, hot dogs 🌭, and popcorn 🍿. You can also get your face painted for free! The fair will be held on the soccer field next to the school. It starts at 4:00 P.M. and finishes at 8:00 P.M. It will last for two days, from June 3 to June 4. Tickets cost four dollars per person. You can buy tickets at the fair or on our website. The money from the fair will help sick children. Come and enjoy the school fair. Bring your friends and family, and you will have a great time!

Q The concluding sentence is the final thought of the passage. Underline the concluding sentence.

B Read the model text again and complete the graphic organizer.

School Fair	
Things to Do	• _____ or play some games • enjoy delicious snacks • get _____ painted for free
Where / When	• on the _____ • starts at 4:00 P.M. and _____ at 8:00 P.M. • from _____
Tickets	• cost _____ per person • can buy them at _____ or on our website
Purpose	help _____

C **Complete the paragraph by using the model text.**

| Title | Announcement: School Fair |

Introduction

Come and join us at _____. There will be fun

for_____.

Body

Things to Do

You can _____.

_____.

You can also _____! The _____

Where

will be _____. It starts at

When

_____ and finishes at _____. It will last for

_____, from _____ to _____.

Tickets

Tickets cost _____ per person. You can buy tickets at

Purpose

_____ or on _____. The money from

the _____ will help _____.

Conclusion

Come and enjoy _____. Bring your _____

_____, and you will have _____!

Collecting Ideas

Look at the example. Fill in the blanks with the phrases in the box.

help the drama club	help local artists	many different sports
~~go on rides~~	have fun in the ice	see live performances

1

School Fair

- on the school soccer field
- <u>go on rides</u>
  or play some games
- help sick children

2

Music Festival

- in Grove Park
- meet musicians and
  _____
- help local homeless people

3

Art Exhibition

- in the school library
- see the art club's artwork
- _____

4

Ice Festival

- at the Spring Resort
- _____ and snow
- help local wildlife

5

Sports Day

- on the school soccer field
- participate in
  _____
- help the school soccer team

6

School Play

- in the school auditorium
- watch some exciting plays
- _____

74

Sentence Practice

A Look at the example and complete the sentences with the words in the box.

~~cotton candy / hot dogs / popcorn~~   pop / jazz / rock

skiing / ice sculpting / skating   sculptures / paintings / drawings

1 Enjoy delicious snacks, **such as** cotton candy, hot dogs, **and** popcorn _____ .

2 Enjoy many kinds of music, _____ .

3 Look at many types of artwork, _____ .

4 Participate in many fun activities, _____ .

B Look at the example and complete the sentences.

Remember to change the verbs to "will be + p.p."

1 (fair / hold on / soccer field)

→ **The** fair **will be held** on **the** soccer field _____ next to the school.

2 (school play / hold in / school auditorium)

→ _____ beside the gym.

3 (music festival / hold in / Grove Park)

→ _____ beside City Hall.

4 (ice festival / hold at / Spring Resort)

→ _____ near Mount Spring.

Your Idea

5 _____

C Look at the example and complete the sentences.

1 two days / June 3 / June 4

→ **It will last for** two days, **from** June 3 **to** June 4.

2 four days / August 10 / August 13

→ _____

3 five days / May 20 / May 24

→ _____

D Look at the pictures. Complete the sentences with the phrases in the box.

local homeless people   ~~sick children~~   the drama club

1 The money from the fair **will help** sick children   .

2 The money from the festival   .

3 The money from the school play   .

E Look at the example and complete the sentences.

1 (friends and family / a great time)

→ **Bring your** friends and family, **and you will have** a great time!

2 (classmates / a wonderful experience)

→ _____

3 (parents / a fantastic evening)

→ _____

Sentence Practice Plus

A **Read the short paragraph. Correct the mistakes and rewrite the sentences.**

Come and join us at the Winter Ice Festival. The ice festival will <u>held</u> at the Spring Resort near Mount Spring. It will last for four days, from January 7 <u>for</u> January 10. <u>Bringing</u> your family, and you <u>have</u> an amazing day!

↓

_____

_____

_____

_____

B **Look at the picture and read the conditions. Write an announcement for the school play like A above.**

Conditions

① Write four sentences.

② Include the following information:
school auditorium – beside the gym / April 10 to April 14 / parents / fantastic evening.

③ Include "will be + p.p." and "imperative, + and ~."

_____

_____

_____

_____

Brainstorming

Write an announcement for a special event. Complete the graphic organizer. Use the ideas in Collecting Ideas or come up with your own.

Announcement: _____	
Things to Do	• • •
Where / When	• • •
Tickets	• •
Purpose	

More Events

Talent Show / Dance Battle / Bake Sale / Science Fair / School Dance / Comedy Show

First Draft

Complete the first draft by using the graphic organizer.

Title

_____

Introduction

Come and join us at _____. There

will be fun for _____.

Body

Things to Do

You can _____.

_____.

You can also _____!

Where

The _____ will be _____.

When

It starts at _____ and finishes at _____. It will

last for _____, from _____ to _____.

Tickets

Tickets cost _____ per person. You can buy tickets

Purpose

_____ or _____. The money from

_____ will help _____.

Conclusion

Come and enjoy _____. Bring your

_____, and you _____!

Unit 8

My Favorite Painting

Writing Goal	Write about your favorite painting.
Type of Writing	Descriptive Writing » Presentation
	Descriptive writing describes a person, place, or thing. It shows what the person, location, or object is like.

Before You Write

A **Read and answer the questions.**

1 Have you ever been to an art gallery?

☐ Yes, I have.   ☐ No, I haven't.

2 Who is your favorite artist?

My favorite artist is _____.

3 What is your favorite painting?

I like _____.

B **Match the pictures with the correct phrases in the box.**

| smiling woman | melting clocks | posing children |
| swirling sky | screaming figure | cloudy sky |

1

2

3

_____   _____   _____

4

5

6

_____   _____   _____

Understanding the Model Text

A Read the model text and answer the question.

The Persistence of Memory

Do you have a favorite painting? My favorite painting is *The Persistence of Memory*. It was painted by Salvador Dali. He made it in 1931. *The Persistence of Memory* is famous for its strange melting clocks. It shows a tree, some cliffs, and a strange monster.

There are watches scattered across the painting. These watches look like they are melting. One of the watches is covered in ants. I like *The Persistence of Memory* because it looks so interesting. The clocks are scary and dream-like. When I see this painting, it makes me feel happy. If you like strange paintings, you should look at *The Persistence of Memory*. You can see this painting in the Museum of Modern Art in New York.

Q The topic sentence is the main idea of the passage. Underline the topic sentence.

B Read the model text again and complete the graphic organizer.

The Persistence of Memory	
Who / When	• painted by _____ • made it in 1931
Famous for	its strange _____

Description	• shows a tree, _____, and a strange monster
	• watches _____ across the painting
	  - look like they are melting
	  - one is covered in _____

Why I Like It	• looks so interesting • clocks are _____ • makes me feel happy

82

C **Complete the paragraph by using the model text.**

Title	*The Persistence of Memory*

Introduction

Do you have a favorite painting? My favorite painting is _____

Who _____. It was painted by _____.

When _____ made it in _____.

Body

Famous for _____ is famous for _____

Description _____. It shows _____

_____. There _____.

_____. _____

Why I Like It _____. I like _____

because _____. The _____

_____. When I see this painting, it makes me

_____.

Conclusion

If you like _____ paintings, you should look at _____

_____. You can see this painting in _____

_____.

Collecting Ideas

Look at the example. Fill in the blanks with the phrases in the box.

> beautiful swirling sky   ~~a strange monster~~   rolling waves
> an orange and yellow sky   her arms crossed   some children

1

The Persistence of Memory

- Salvador Dali / 1931
- strange melting clocks
- shows a tree, some cliffs, and

  <u>a strange monster</u>

2

The Starry Night

- Vincent van Gogh / 1889
- _____
- shows a city, some hills, and the night sky

3

Mona Lisa

- Leonardo da Vinci / 1503
- mysterious smiling woman
- shows a woman sitting with

  _____

4

A Stormy Sea

- Claude Monet / 1883
- _____
- shows a sea and a cloudy sky

5

The Scream

- Edvard Munch / 1893
- screaming figure
- shows a bridge and

  _____

6

Three Children with a Dog

- Sofonisba Anguissola / 1590
- posing children
- shows _____ and a small dog

Sentence Practice

A **Look at the example and complete the sentences.**

> (*The Persistence of Memory*) → Its strange clocks <u>are melting</u>.
> → *The Persistence of Memory* **is famous for** its strange **melting** clocks.

💡 Place the underlined words before the noun and remove the be verb.

1 (*The Starry Night*) → Its beautiful sky <u>is swirling</u>.

→ _____

2 (The *Mona Lisa*) → Its mysterious woman <u>is smiling</u>.

→ _____

3 (*The Scream*) → Its figure <u>is screaming</u>.

→ _____

4 (*A Stormy Sea*) → Its waves <u>are rolling</u>.

→ _____

Your Idea

5 _____

B **Look at the example and rewrite the sentences.**

1 There are watches. The watches are scattered across the painting.

→ There are watches **scattered** across the painting.

2 There are many circles. The circles are scattered across the sky.

→ _____

3 There are three children. The children are posing with their dog.

→ _____

4 There are many colors. The colors are swirling across the sky.

→ _____

C Look at the pictures. Complete the sentences with the phrases in the box.

| ~~these watches~~   these circles   this figure | stars at night   a skull   ~~they are melting~~ |

1 These watches **look like** they are melting. _____

2 _____

3 _____

D Look at the example and complete the sentences.

1 *The Persistence of Memory* / interesting

→ **I like** *The Persistence of Memory* **because it looks so** interesting. _____

2 *The Starry Night* / dreamy

→ _____

3 *The Scream* / scary and mysterious

→ _____

E Look at the example and rewrite the sentences.

1 You like strange paintings. Look at *The Persistence of Memory*.

→ **If** you like strange paintings, **you should** look at *The Persistence of Memory*. _____

2 You like beautiful paintings. Look at *The Starry Night*.

→ _____

3 You like unique paintings. Look at *Three Children with a Dog*.

→ _____

Sentence Practice ^{Plus}

Ⓐ Read the short paragraph. Correct the mistakes and rewrite the sentences.

My favorite painting <u>are</u> the *Mona Lisa*. It was <u>paint</u> by Leonardo da Vinci. The *Mona Lisa* is famous for its mysterious <u>smiles</u> woman. The woman <u>looks</u> she feels both happy and sad.

_____

_____

_____

_____

Ⓑ Look at the picture and read the conditions. Write about *A Stormy Sea* like A above.

Conditions

① Write four sentences.

② Include the following information: Claude Monet / roll – waves / these clouds – cotton candy.

③ Include a present participle and "look like."

_____

_____

_____

_____

Brainstorming

Write about your favorite painting. Complete the graphic organizer. Use the ideas in Collecting Ideas or come up with your own.

Who / When	• •
Famous for	
Description	• • — —
Why I Like It	• • •

More Paintings

The Lady of Shalott by John William Waterhouse (1888) / *The Kiss* by Gustav Klimt (1908)
Ssireum (Korean Wrestling) by Kim Hong-do (late 18th century) / *Geumgang Jeondo* by Jeong Seon (1734)

First Draft

Complete the first draft by using the graphic organizer.

Title

_____

Introduction

Do you have a favorite painting? My favorite painting is _____

Who

_____. It was painted by _____.

When

_____ made it in _____.

Body

Famous for

_____ is famous for _____.

Description

It shows _____.

There _____.

_____.

_____.

Why I Like It

I like _____ because _____.

_____.

When I see this painting, it makes me _____.

Conclusion

If you like _____ paintings, you should look at _____

_____. You can see this painting in _____

_____.

Vocabulary & Structure Review

Unit 1
My Favorite Time of Day

Read the words and phrases. Write the meaning next to each word and phrase.

1	filmmaking		11	calm	
2	shoot		12	gym	
3	edit		13	cafeteria	
4	huge		14	match (*n.*)	
5	squirrel		15	telescope	
6	fountain		16	planet	
7	film (*n., v.*)		17	meteor	
8	chase		18	cheer	
9	outdoors (↔ indoors)		19	get ready for	
10	relaxing		20	wait for	

Structures

1 watch / hear / see + object + verb

e.g I <u>watch the squirrels chase</u> one another and then film them.
I <u>hear my friends cheer</u> for me.

2 while + subject + verb

e.g I go home and edit my videos <u>while I wait</u> for dinner.

Unit 2
The Worst Day of My Life

Read the words and phrases. Write the meaning next to each word and phrase.

1	terrible		11	gross	
2	miss		12	bite (*n.*)	
3	realize		13	wallet	
4	scold		14	fight (fought-fought)	
5	embarrassed		15	forget	
6	frustrated		16	knee	
7	disappointed		17	fall off	
8	hide		18	set one's alarm	
9	lunchtime (*cf.* dinnertime)		19	to make matters worse (= what is worse)	
10	serve		20	get better	

Structures

1 so + adjective + that + subject + verb

> e.g I felt <u>so</u> embarrassed <u>that</u> I wanted to hide.

2 the past continuous tense: was / were + verb-ing

> e.g My school cafeteria <u>was serving</u> gross ham sandwiches.

Unit 3
School Lunches Around the World

Read the words and phrases. Write the meaning next to each word and phrase.

1	healthy		11	full	
2	nutritious		12	baked goods	
3	meat (*cf.* beef)		13	side dish	
4	vegetable		14	grilled	
5	dessert		15	tofu	
6	tray		16	cutlet	
7	cucumber		17	cover (*v.*)	
8	cabbage		18	be made with	
9	bean (*cf.* pea)		19	be ready to	
10	tasty		20	such as (= like)	

Structures

1 to-infinitive of purpose

e.g In France, students eat nutritious foods <u>to stay</u> healthy.

2 the relative pronoun "that"

e.g For example, they might have fish, sausages, or beef <u>that</u> is covered in sauce.

Unit 4
The Most Popular Pets

Read the words and phrases. Write the meaning next to each word and phrase.

1	pet		11	slimy	
2	classmate		12	furry	
3	vote (*v.*)		13	least (↔ most)	
4	result		14	walk (*v.*)	
5	survey		15	feed	
6	friendly		16	rest (*n.*)	
7	playful		17	quiet	
8	popular		18	boring (↔ interesting)	
9	noisy		19	cage	
10	scary		20	take care of	

Structures

1 superlative adjectives: the + -est / most + adjective

e.g They said dogs are <u>the friendliest</u> and <u>most</u> playful pets.

2 adjective + to-infinitive

e.g Nine students like cats the best because they are <u>easy to take care of</u>.

Unit 5
The Best Place to Travel

Read the words and phrases. Write the meaning next to each word and phrase.

1	suggest		11	try (v.)	
2	visit		12	steamed	
3	landmark		13	photograph (n., v.)	
4	temple		14	contest	
5	sunrise		15	sculpture	
6	sunset		16	rock formation	
7	market		17	arena	
8	palace		18	take a trip	
9	museum		19	go on a tour	
10	crowded		20	take part in (= participate in)	

Structures

1 the present perfect tense: have / has + p.p.

e.g I have been there once with my parents.

2 suggest (+ that) + subject (+ should) + verb

e.g I suggest you visit Cambodia.

Unit 6
Save the Environment

Read the words and phrases. Write the meaning next to each word and phrase.

1	pollution		11	leftovers	
2	save		12	properly	
3	reduce		13	reusable	
4	garbage		14	food waste	
5	recycle		15	public transportation	
6	separate (*v.*)		16	grocery store	
7	own (*a.*)		17	turn off (← turn on)	
8	environment		18	in addition	
9	amount		19	take notes	
10	lower (*v.*)		20	put away	

Structures

1 remember to + verb

e.g Remember to turn off computers and televisions if you aren't using them.

2 omission of the relative pronoun "that"

e.g First, you should reduce the amount of garbage you make.

(= garbage that you make)

Unit 7
Join Us at the Fair

Read the words and phrases. Write the meaning next to each word and phrase.

1	fair		11	last (v.)	
2	festival		12	cost (v.)	
3	exhibition		13	live (a.)	
4	announcement		14	performance	
5	whole (a.)		15	homeless	
6	cotton candy		16	artwork	
7	hold (held-held)		17	wildlife	
8	soccer field		18	for free	
9	auditorium		19	per person	
10	local		20	go on rides	

Structures

1 **will be + p.p.**

   e.g The fair <u>will be held</u> on the soccer field next to the school.

2 **imperative, + and ~**

   e.g <u>Bring</u> your friends and family, <u>and</u> you will have a great time!

98

Unit 8
My Favorite Painting

Read the words and phrases. Write the meaning next to each word and phrase.

1	painting		11	rolling	
2	paint (*v.*)		12	screaming	
3	memory		13	pose (*v.*)	
4	persistence		14	scatter	
5	cliff		15	monster	
6	dream-like (= dreamy)		16	wave	
7	unique		17	figure	
8	mysterious		18	modern art	
9	melting		19	look like	
10	swirling		20	be famous for	

Structures

1 past participle (-ed) / present participle (-ing)

e.g There are watches <u>scattered</u> across the painting.

The Persistence of Memory is famous for its strange <u>melting</u> clocks.

2 "look like" + noun / clause

e.g These circles <u>look like stars</u> at night.

These watches <u>look like they are melting.</u>

Memo

Memo

Memo

Memo

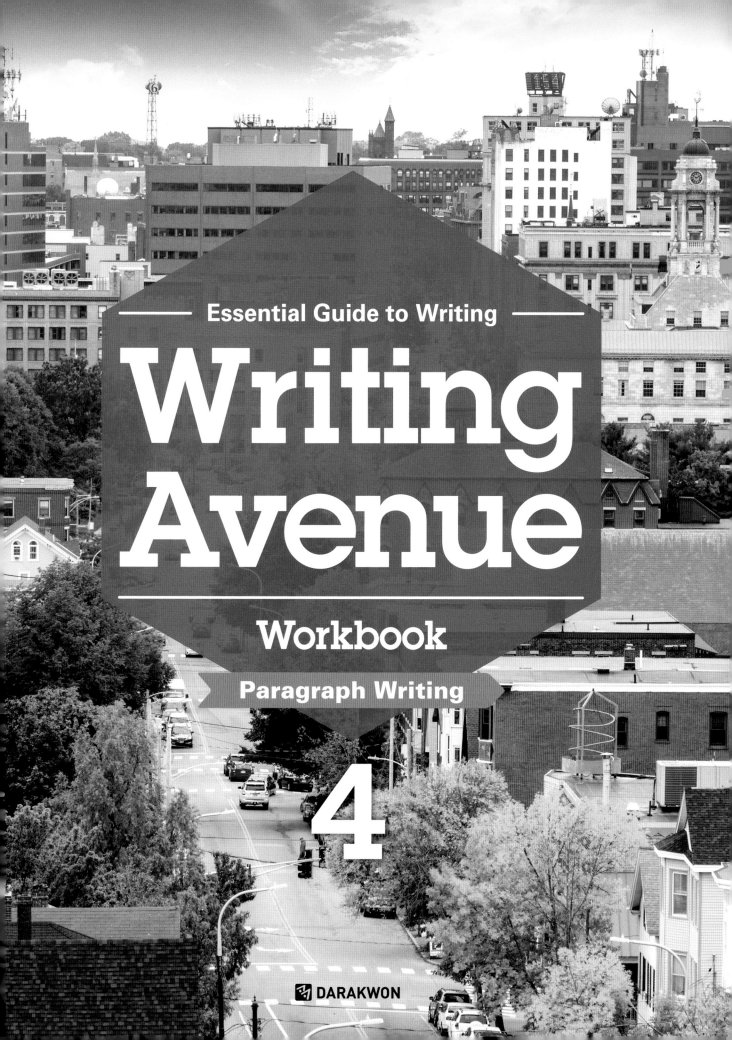

Essential Guide to Writing

Writing Avenue

Workbook

Paragraph Writing

4

DARAKWON

Unit 1 My Favorite Time of Day

A **Look at the example and complete the sentences.**

1 edit my videos / wait for dinner

→ I edit my videos **while** I wait for dinner.

2 take a shower / my mom makes breakfast

→ _____

3 listen to music / walk home from school

→ _____

4 think about my day / get ready for bed

→ _____

B **Look at the example and rewrite the sentences.**

1 I watch the squirrels. They chase one another.

→ I **watch** the squirrels **chase** one another.

2 I watch the basketball players. They shoot the ball.

→ _____

3 I hear the children. They shout at one another.

→ _____

4 I watch the rabbits. They hop in the gardens.

→ _____

C **Match the phrases. Then, write the sentences.**

1	There is a huge park with •	•	being outdoors
2	When the weather is nice, •	•	while I wait for dinner
3	I learn •	•	between 3:00 and 5:00 P.M.
4	I watch the squirrels •	•	many trees, gardens, and fountains near my school
5	I really enjoy •	•	chase one another and then film them
6	My favorite time of day is •	•	have such a relaxing afternoon
7	I'm glad to •	•	how to shoot and edit short films there
8	I go home and edit my videos •	•	our film teacher, Mr. Sparks, takes us outside

1 _____

2 _____

3 _____

4 _____

5 _____

6 _____

7 _____

8 _____

Revise & Edit

Write about your favorite time of day. Refer to the First Draft in the student book. Then, edit your paragraph.

Title

Introduction

Body

Conclusion

Editing Checklist ☐ Capitalization   ☐ Punctuation   ☐ Grammar   ☐ Spelling

Final Draft

Write the final draft.

Title

Unit 2 The Worst Day of My Life

A **Look at the example and rewrite the sentences.**

1 My school cafeteria served gross ham sandwiches.

→ My school cafeteria **was serving** gross ham sandwiches.

2 My soccer team lost the match.

→ _____

3 My friends had gross sushi for lunch.

→ _____

4 I waited for my friend for an hour.

→ _____

B **Look at the example. Unscramble the words to complete the sentences.**

1 so embarrassed / I wanted / I felt / to hide / that

→ I felt so embarrassed that I wanted to hide. _____

2 to cry / I felt / that / I wanted / so upset

→ _____

3 that / to run away / so annoyed / I felt / I wanted

→ _____

4 to scream / I felt / I wanted / so frustrated / that

→ _____

C **Match the phrases. Then, write the sentences.**

1	Yesterday was the worst	•	• in front of the class
2	I woke up late	•	• better by lunchtime
3	My teacher scolded me	•	• day of my life
4	To make matters worse, I lost	•	• I forgot my math book
5	My day didn't get	•	• a day like that again
6	I couldn't eat a bite,	•	• because I forgot to set my alarm
7	I really hope I never have	•	• so I was hungry all afternoon
8	When I got to school, I realized	•	• my favorite wallet on the way home

1 _____

2 _____

3 _____

4 _____

5 _____

6 _____

7 _____

8 _____

Revise & Edit

**Write about a terrible day. Refer to the First Draft in the student book.
Then, edit your paragraph.**

Title	

Introduction

Body

Conclusion

Editing Checklist ☐ Capitalization ☐ Punctuation ☐ Grammar ☐ Spelling

Final Draft

Write the final draft.

Title

Unit 3 School Lunches Around the World

A **Look at the example. Unscramble the words to complete the sentences.**

> (students / nutritious foods / in France, / healthy / to stay / eat)
> → In France, students eat nutritious foods to stay healthy.

1 (eat / in Ukraine, / to stay / big lunches / full / students)

→ _____

2 (to stay / in South Korea, / healthy foods / students / strong / eat)

→ _____

3 (students / to stay / in Colombia, / nutritious foods / eat / healthy)

→ _____

4 (in the U.S., / eat / delicious foods / full all afternoon / to stay / students)

→ _____

B **Look at the example and rewrite the sentences.**

1 They might have fish, sausages, or beef. The beef is covered in sauce.

→ They might have fish, sausages, or beef **that** is covered in sauce.

2 They might have fish, fried chicken, or pork. The pork is covered in sauce.

→ _____

3 They might have meatballs, chicken, or plantains. The plantains are fried in oil.

→ _____

4 They might have carrots, peas, broccoli, or beans. The beans are cooked in sauce.

→ _____

C **Match the phrases. Then, write the sentences.**

1	After lunch, they feel full,	•	•	on a tray
2	The food is served	•	•	in the school cafeteria
3	The salad is made	•	•	for lunch at school
4	Sometimes they have fruit,	•	•	that is covered in sauce
5	They have lunch	•	•	such as apples or peaches
6	What do you normally eat	•	•	like ice cream, cake, or apple pie
7	Other times they eat something sweet,	•	•	and they are ready to study again
8	For example, they might have fish, sausages, or beef	•	•	with cucumbers, cabbage, and tomatoes

1 _____

2 _____

3 _____

4 _____

5 _____

6 _____

7 _____

8 _____

Revise & Edit

Write about school lunch in another country. Refer to the First Draft in the student book. Then, edit your paragraph.

Title	

Introduction

Body

Conclusion

Editing Checklist ☐ Capitalization ☐ Punctuation ☐ Grammar ☐ Spelling

Final Draft

Write the final draft.

Title

Unit 4 The Most Popular Pets

A **Circle the mistakes and rewrite the sentences.**

1 They said dogs are (friendlier) and most playful pets.

→ They said dogs are **the friendliest** and most playful pets.

2 They said rabbits are the cutest and interesting pets.

→ _____

3 They said fish are the cheapest and most pretty pets.

→ _____

4 They said cats are smartest and fastest pets.

→ _____

B **Look at the example and complete the sentences.**

1 (nine / cats) (easy / take care of)

→ Nine **students like** cats **the best because they are** easy **to** take care of.

2 (eleven / hamsters) (easy / feed)

→ _____

3 (seven / dogs) (easy / teach)

→ _____

4 (ten / iguanas) (their cages / easy / clean)

→ _____

14

C **Match the phrases. Then, write the sentences.**

1 Cats are the second •   • wants a pet

2 This chart shows that •   • most popular pets

3 You don't need to walk •   • and most playful pets

4 I asked my classmates •   • a cat or play with it a lot

5 Everyone in my class •   • which pets they like the most

6 Most students don't like hamsters • • are scary and difficult to feed

7 The rest of the class said snakes • • fifteen students voted for dogs

8 They said dogs are the friendliest • • because they are noisy at night

1 _____

2 _____

3 _____

4 _____

5 _____

6 _____

7 _____

8 _____

Revise & Edit

Write about your classmates' favorite pets. Refer to the First Draft in the student book. Then, edit your paragraph.

Title

Introduction

Body

Conclusion

Editing Checklist ☐ Capitalization ☐ Punctuation ☐ Grammar ☐ Spelling

Final Draft

Write the final draft.

Title

Unit 5 The Best Place to Travel

A **Look at the pictures. Complete the sentences with the phrases in the box.**

> ~~visit Cambodia~~   take part in the sand sculpture contest
> try the fresh lobster   photograph the rock formations

1 **I suggest you** visit Cambodia. _____

2 _____

3 _____

4 _____

B **Look at the example and rewrite the sentences.**

1 I went there once. (my parents)

→ I **have been** there once **with** my parents. _____

2 I went there twice. (my family)

→ _____

3 I went there a few times. (my aunt)

→ _____

4 I visited the museum four times. (my brother)

→ _____

C **Match the phrases. Then, write the sentences.**

1 I suggest   •

2 It took all day   •

3 That's the best time to   •

4 While I was there,   •

5 We saw a lot of beautiful   •

6 It is one of the most   •

7 It is the most crowded   •

8 You should go there at   •

• I visited Angkor Wat

• sunrise or sunset

• you try the fish amok

• market in Phnom Penh

• temples there

• take photographs

• to walk through the park

• famous landmarks in Cambodia

1 _____

2 _____

3 _____

4 _____

5 _____

6 _____

7 _____

8 _____

Revise & Edit

Recommend a place to go on vacation. Refer to the First Draft in the student book. Then, edit your paragraph.

Title

Introduction

Body

Conclusion

Editing Checklist ☐ Capitalization ☐ Punctuation ☐ Grammar ☐ Spelling

Final Draft

Write the final draft.

Title

Unit 6 Save the Environment

A **Look at the example and complete the sentences.**

1 | reduce / amount / garbage / make |

→ **You should** reduce **the** amount **of** garbage **you** make. _____

2 | reduce / amount / food / waste |

→ _____

3 | reduce / amount / air pollution / make |

→ _____

4 | reduce / amount / plastic / throw away |

→ _____

B **Look at the pictures. Complete the sentences with the phrases in the box.**

| ~~turn off computers and televisions~~ take shorter showers, too bring a reusable bottle or cup to school use natural shampoos and soaps |

1 **Remember to** turn off computers and televisions. _____

2 _____

3 _____

4 _____

C **Match the phrases. Then, write the sentences.**

1	Let's help	•	•	all over the world
2	Why don't you bring	•	•	save our Earth
3	When you leave a room,	•	•	turn off the lights
4	These are just two ways	•	•	before you put it outside
5	Pollution is a big problem	•	•	you can help the environment
6	In winter, lower the heat	•	•	your own bags when you shop
7	Wash and separate your recycling	•	•	as much as possible
8	To do that, you should recycle	•	•	and put on a sweater

1 _____

2 _____

3 _____

4 _____

5 _____

6 _____

7 _____

8 _____

Revise & Edit

Write about two ways to save the environment. Refer to the First Draft in the student book. Then, edit your paragraph.

Title	
Introduction	
Body	
Conclusion	

Editing Checklist ☐ Capitalization ☐ Punctuation ☐ Grammar ☐ Spelling

Final Draft

Write the final draft.

Title

Unit 7 Join Us at the Fair

A **Look at the example and rewrite the sentences.**

1 | The fair is on the soccer field. It is next to the school. |

→ The fair **will be held** on the soccer field next to the school.

2 | Sports day is on the soccer field. It is beside the parking lot. |

→ _____

3 | The school play is in the auditorium. It is beside the gym. |

→ _____

4 | The ice festival is at the Spring Resort. It is near Mount Spring. |

→ _____

B **Look at the example. Unscramble the words to complete the sentences.**

1 (your friends, / bring / you will / and / a great time / have)

→ **Bring your friends, and you will have a great time!**

2 (your classmates, / and / you will / bring / a great time / have)

→ _____

3 (bring / and / an amazing experience / your parents, / you will / have)

→ _____

4 (your whole family, / have / bring / and / you will / a wonderful evening)

→ _____

C Match the phrases. Then, write the sentences.

1	Tickets cost	•		•	at the Oak School Fair
2	You can also get your face	•		•	will help sick children
3	Come and join us	•		•	from June 3 to June 4
4	It starts at 4:00 P.M.	•		•	four dollars per person
5	There will be fun	•		•	and finishes at 8:00 P.M.
6	It will last for two days,	•		•	painted for free
7	The money from the fair	•		•	at the fair or on our website
8	You can buy tickets	•		•	for the whole family

1 _____

2 _____

3 _____

4 _____

5 _____

6 _____

7 _____

8 _____

Revise & Edit

Write an announcement for a special event. Refer to the First Draft in the student book. Then, edit your paragraph.

Title

Introduction

Body

Conclusion

Editing Checklist ☐ Capitalization ☐ Punctuation ☐ Grammar ☐ Spelling

Final Draft

Write the final draft.

Title

Unit 8 My Favorite Painting

A **Look at the example. Underline the mistake in each sentence and rewrite the sentences.**

1 *The Persistence of Memory* is famous for its strange <u>melt</u> clocks.

→ *The Persistence of Memory* is famous for its strange **melting** clocks.

2 *The Scream* is famous for its screamed figure.

→ _____

3 *A Stormy Sea* is famous for its roll waves.

→ _____

4 The *Mona Lisa* is famous for its mysterious smile woman.

→ _____

B **Look at the example and rewrite the sentences.**

1 I like *The Persistence of Memory*. It is interesting.

→ I like *The Persistence of Memory* **because it looks so** interesting.

2 I like the *Mona Lisa*. It is peaceful.

→ _____

3 I like *The Scream*. It is unique.

→ _____

4 I like *The Starry Night*. It is dreamy.

→ _____

30

C **Match the phrases. Then, write the sentences.**

1 It was painted · · they are melting

2 One of the watches · · by Salvador Dali

3 You can see this painting · · is covered in ants

4 These watches look like · · it makes me feel happy

5 When I see this painting, · · for its strange melting clocks

6 There are watches · · scattered across the painting

7 If you like strange paintings, · · in the Museum of Modern Art in New York

8 *The Persistence of Memory* is famous · · you should look at *The Persistence of Memory*

1 _____

2 _____

3 _____

4 _____

5 _____

6 _____

7 _____

8 _____

Revise & Edit

Write about your favorite painting. Refer to the First Draft in the student book. Then, edit your paragraph.

Title	

Introduction

Body

Conclusion

Editing Checklist ☐ Capitalization ☐ Punctuation ☐ Grammar ☐ Spelling

Final Draft

Write the final draft.

Title

Memo

Essential Guide to Writing

Writing Avenue

Paragraph Writing

Essential Guide to Writing

Writing Avenue

Paragraph Writing

4

• Writing Avenue Series

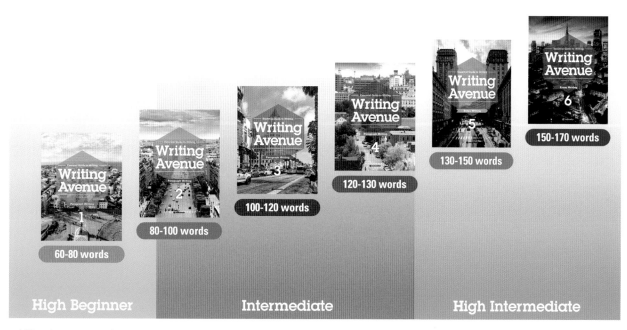

| Paragraph Writing | | | | Essay Writing | |

6
150-170 words

5
130-150 words

4
120-130 words

3
100-120 words

2
80-100 words

1
60-80 words

High Beginner   **Intermediate**   **High Intermediate**

* Word counts refer to the length of the model texts.

Essential Guide to Writing

Writing Avenue

Paragraph Writing

4

Writing Avenue is a six-level writing series divided into two stages: paragraph writing and essay writing. The series is designed for high-beginner to high-intermediate students. Writing Avenue covers four types of writing and various topics ranging from daily life to social issues. By going through a series of steps, students can improve their writing skills and eventually transition from writing paragraphs to writing essays.

Features

- Guided steps to help plan and complete the writing
- Vocabulary preview related to each topic
- Model text serving as an example for each topic
- Graphic organizers to help organize and outline ideas
- Brainstorming section with additional concepts and ideas
- Key sentence structures and patterns related to each topic
- Various formats to practice different types of writing assignments
- Workbook providing extra sentence practice

Components

Student Book / Workbook

Download Resources   www.darakwon.co.kr

MP3 files / Answer key / Translations / Vocabulary lists / Vocabulary tests / Translation worksheets / Review tests

Scan this QR code for online resources

Writing Avenue Series

54740

₩ 14,500

9788927704508

ISBN 978-89-277-0450-8
ISBN 978-89-277-0446-1 (set)

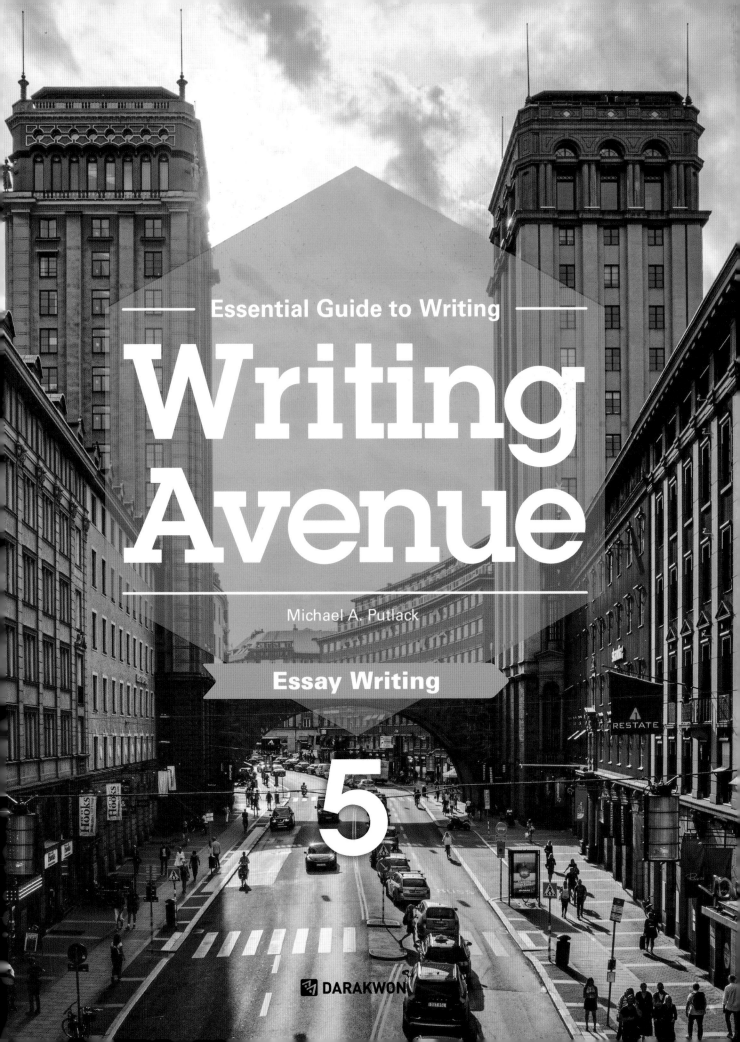